A COACHING MINDSET

Introducing The Ultimate
Superpower For Managers & Supervisors

Keith E. Smith

StraightUpLiving.com

Copyright © 2024 Keith E. Smith

All rights reserved. No part of this book may be reproduced, stored in a retrieval system, or transmitted in any form or media or by any means, electronic, mechanical, photocopying, recording, or otherwise, without the prior written permission of the authors, except in the case of brief quotations embodied in critical articles and reviews.

ISBN: 9798322134565

Table of Contents

01 Introduction

05 What is Coaching?

09 How is Coaching and Management Different?

14 Merging Management and Coaching

27 Benefits of a Coaching Style of Leadership

40 Common Challenges Transitioning to a Coaching Style

46 Everyone Has a Social Style

55 Active Listening and Why It's a Crucial Skill

59 Why Caring Leadership Matters

72 5 Hot Tips for Developing a Coaching Mindset

74 Coaching Questions Examples

76 Assessing Your Coaching Mindset

83 You Make a Bigger Difference Than You Think

87 Recommended Reading

> "If you want to build a ship, don't drum up the men to gather wood, divide the work, and give orders. Instead, teach them to yearn for the vast and endless sea."

Antoine de Saint-Exupéry

Introduction

In my early days of management, I had to learn to handle more than just myself. While I had excelled as an employee and received frequent recognition for my achievements, I found that few of the skills I possessed translated to management. Regardless of the industry I was in—automotive, construction, or health and wellness—I tried every technique I could think of, but to no avail.

Years later, things finally started falling into place. While co-managing a health and wellness business, I was given the challenge of increasing monthly memberships (therapeutic massage studio) to at least 600. This was a significant jump from the low 500s where it had stagnated for years. That meant transforming our non-salespeople at the front desk into effective sales staff. Additionally, I was tasked with reducing the horrendous employee turnover rate. Once again, I attempted to implement various tactics, including:

- Cheerleading/pep talks.

- Sales scripts.
- One-on-one meetings.
- Tracking sales ratios.
- Hard work.
- Role playing.
- Hiring new people.
- Sales goals.

Nothing I tried had a significant or lasting effect, and I was burning out. Sound familiar? If you've been a manager for a long time, I bet you're nodding your head right now. But the story doesn't end there, in fact it was the beginning of a whole new mindset for me. What turned things around? Self-awareness: my approach wasn't working, and that was on me, not my team.

I realized the people I worked with were more than capable, their potential just hadn't been unleashed. I began shifting my mindset and approach. I started collaborating with my people. They were given more autonomy, instead of being assigned tasks or pre-programmed processes. I changed my style of communication by learning theirs. I was transparent about any changes being made and asked for feedback.

In other words, I adopted a more coaching-oriented attitude rather than a pure managerial one.

At the time, I didn't recognize it as coaching; it was simply an instinctual shift in my approach. The spark that ignited the change happened after I discovered something called Social Styles, which we'll cover later, but basically, it's how we communicate with others, and the way we prefer others to communicate with us.

It took time, and it wasn't perfect, but the atmosphere transformed. Everyone was happier at work and made more money too. Employee turnover all but vanished and more than 200 members were added in less than 18 months, and that's factoring in attrition rates which fell sharply. Not bad for a six-room studio.

It was a great example of what's possible when a workplace takes on a coaching atmosphere. People felt seen and heard because they WERE seen and heard. Growth followed naturally, and they all tapped into their own potential. Another interesting tidbit: everything on the "didn't work list" above? They all worked AFTER the transformation.

My conclusion is this: tactics, training, and techniques have little impact if people do not feel acknowledged and valued, or if they perceive management as uncaring.

Previously, I focused on addressing the symptoms (low sales, attrition, employee turnover) rather than tackling the root cause. I realized we had great people; they just needed to be activated. Coaching is what made the difference.

Coaching isn't just an attractive option or something that's nice to have. It's now an essential, must-have skill for all managers and business leaders. If you're a manager or supervisor, I want you to know that you have the power to activate hope in your people. There's no need to hand out insincere or shallow compliments. Nor is there a need to draw undo attention to mistakes or rule with an iron fist. These things will only hinder your progress and alienate others. All you need is empathy, a genuine desire to help others succeed, and a willingness to change. If you embody these traits, I believe you will naturally transition into a Coaching Manager.

Chapter One
What is Coaching?

In today's ever-changing business landscape, your role as a manager is quickly evolving. Traditional management approaches, which tend to be focused on control and direction, are giving way to a more collaborative style of leadership that is far more effective: coaching.

Coaching is simply a conversation, or a series of conversations, with another person. What makes a coaching conversation different is the effect the conversation has on the individual being coached. A coaching conversation influences someone's behavior, understanding, and progress. It's a collaborative and empowering process that helps individuals unlock their full potential, create and achieve meaningful goals, and overcome internal and external obstacles.

Unlike a traditional management approach, that relies on authority and direction, coaching focuses on asking questions, active listening, and giving support and guidance to help individuals find their own solutions. Coaching isn't about telling people exactly what to do or solving their problems for them. Instead, it's about empowering individuals to think critically, explore new perspectives, and take ownership of their development and success.

A coach isn't a boss or mentor, they're a guide—a facilitator of growth and learning. A coach helps their team members set goals that are meaningful to them as individuals and helps them overcome obstacles along the way. One of the primary goals of a coach is establishing a relationship built on trust and mutual respect. In a coaching relationship, you're less of a boss and more of a partner, working alongside team members and helping them identify their strengths, overcome challenges, and achieve their objectives.

Coaching Isn't Training

I've talked to a lot of managers and business leaders, and there are two things I've heard many times when the subject of coaching comes up:

1. "Oh, I'm already coaching my team." But what they really mean is that they're mentoring their people or they're just really nice when telling them what to do.

2. "My team needs this." The implication being that they don't need it, but their people do.

These responses often indicate a lack of self-awareness. Please understand, mentoring is great and a valuable way to pass on knowledge and experience, it just isn't coaching. Being nice is also good, but it isn't coaching either. But when I hear someone effectively say, "I don't need this" I know I'm probably dealing with a fixed mindset. A fixed mindset isn't flexible and leaves little room for growth, and I find it almost heartbreaking when a leader sees no value in their own development.

Leaders who think their team "needs this" typically view coaching as a form of training, which isn't accurate. As previously mentioned, coaching is an intentional conversation built on mutual respect and trust. Instead of just one person holding and sharing the knowledge, coaching is a collaborative experience where the people involved come together to find solutions and devise a plan to implement them. Even when a coach is guiding the conversation, their intent is to help the other person arrive at a solution and a plan of action. The aim of coaching is helping people think for themselves.

An important distinction to make between a coaching manager and a coach is this: although a coaching manager will ask questions and engage in active listening instead of automatically entering into " fix it" mode, there are times when they'll have to offer direction. Someone who is just a coach may not do this, but there are certain situations when a manager will have to step in and offer specific directions.

For example, if you've just hired a new employee and they come to you with a question on their first day, no amount of coaching will draw the answer out of them. It's their first day on the job and they're not yet familiar with their role. In other words, they don't know what they don't know. In that situation they would need specific answers and direction. As the new employee develops and grows into their role, you can adjust your approach so that it leans more toward a coaching style. The ability to recognize when to adjust your approach will be an invaluable skill for you to develop as a leader.

The goal of this book is to provide you with enough knowledge and tools to help you adopt a coaching style of leadership and understand how and why it'll make you a more effective and successful leader.

Chapter Two

How is Coaching and Managing Different?

Coaching is a collaborative and empowering process that focuses on unlocking an individual's potential, fostering their growth, and helping them achieve their goals. Unlike managing, which often involves directing and controlling, coaching is about guiding and supporting individuals to find their own solutions, develop their skills, and take ownership of their personal and professional development. A coach will never claim to have all the answers. Their purpose is to help you find the answers yourself.

One of the key aspects of coaching is the emphasis on asking powerful questions. Coaches use questions to help people more deeply explore their thoughts, feelings, and perspectives, which can lead to deeper insights and self-discovery. By encouraging an individual to think critically and reflect on their experiences, coaches help empower them to make informed decisions and take action.

Another aspect of coaching, and perhaps the most important, is active listening. A coach listens not only to what is being said, but also to what is not being said. By tuning into nonverbal cues and underlying emotions, coaches can gain a deeper understanding of the individual's challenges and provide more meaningful support. One reason for this is that people will often want something on a deeper level, but the words they use to express it may seem unrelated.

Coaching is about empowering people to excel, both personally and professionally. A coaching relationship is a partnership built on respect, mutual understanding, trust, and with the goal of helping someone reach their full potential.

In contrast, **managing** is more about overseeing tasks, projects, and operations to ensure that a company's objectives are met. As a manager, you're responsible for directing and controlling resources, allocating tasks, and achieving predefined outcomes. While managing also involves supporting and developing employees, the primary focus is on achieving specific goals and targets set by the organization.

Managers typically use a more directive approach, providing clear instructions and guidance to ensure that tasks are completed as desired. While this approach can be effective in certain situations, it can also be limiting, as it may not fully leverage the skills, creativity, and potential of individual team members. The old adage, "Two heads are better than one" is true. If you don't tap into the skills, knowledge, and experience of the people on your team, then everything depends on you. Even if you're one of the most experienced and skilled managers on Earth, you're reducing the odds of success if you ignore the capabilities of other people.

Another difference between coaching and managing is the focus on individual development. While managing is more about achieving specific outcomes, coaching is about helping individuals grow and develop in a way that is meaningful to them. This can lead to more engaged, motivated, and fulfilled employees, which will benefit everyone. I think that deserves to be repeated: **everyone will benefit from a coaching atmosphere.** Not just the business or certain employees.

Simply put, managers typically use a direct approach. This style involves a more authoritative style of relating to people. A manager tells employees what to do, how to do it, and when to do it. Decisions are usually made by the manager, and there's less room for employees to offer their input or work with autonomy.

A coach uses a more non-direct approach. This style is more collaborative and facilitative. They help guide individuals through decision-making and problem-solving processes rather than dictating solutions to them. They encourage people to take ownership of their work, develop their skills, and find creative solutions to obstacles or challenges.

A Few Key Points

- **Control vs. Empowerment:** A traditional management style tends to focus on controlling actions and outcomes, while coaching emphasizes empowering employees to make decisions, arrive at their own conclusions, and take ownership of their work.

- **Problem-solving vs. Development:** Managers will often focus on solving an immediate problem, whereas a coach will make it a priority to develop an employee's skills and capabilities.

- **Directive vs. Facilitative:** Traditional managers usually give directives and specific instructions. A coach will first ask questions, truly listen, and provide guidance to help employees find their own solutions.

- **Short-term vs. Long-term**: Generally speaking, traditional management focuses on short-term results, while coaching looks at long-term development and growth.

Chapter Three
Merging Management and Coaching

There are organizations who are recognizing the value of coaching in developing their leadership and are beginning to integrate the principles of coaching into their management practices. This merging of coaching and management represents a new (and much needed) leadership standard, where leaders are not just managers and mentors, but also coaches who facilitate a genuine environment of support and learning. This approach is far more inclusive, empowering, and effective, because it leverages the strengths of both coaching and managing to create a more agile and innovative role: The Coaching Manager.

A coaching manager isn't just focused on achieving specific outcomes but also on developing their teams and building a more positive culture of continuous learning and improvement. They help create a workplace culture where people feel safe and aren't afraid of making mistakes because their coaching manager has made it clear (through their words and behaviors) that mistakes are a normal and expected part of the learning process.

These are core values of a coaching mindset, which is all about believing in the potential of others and helping them believe in that potential too. It's about seeing each team member as a unique individual with their own strengths, weaknesses, and aspirations.

There are several core values that underpin a coaching mindset, including empathy, curiosity, and a belief in the inherent intelligence and abilities of your team members. When you adopt and embody these values, you can expect to experience a wide range of benefits, both for yourself and the people you're working with. Increased sense of purpose and engagement, higher levels of morale and job satisfaction, and even lower rates of employee turnover.

Let's be real. This is going to involve some work. It isn't all that complicated, and you're certainly more than capable of seeing it through, but doing so is going to require three things:

1. Effort
2. Self-discipline
3. Consistency

This isn't a process you'll have down in a week or even a month. In fact, don't even think of it as a process or a tactic. It's a lifestyle. This is a way of being and you'll have to be committed to showing up every day.

Why Do We Need Coaches in Business?

Regardless of the size of the business, managers face numerous challenges. High turnover rates, increased stress, overwhelmed employees, and the realization that the "same old way" of doing things just doesn't work. Coaching offers a way forward by addressing these challenges and creating a more engaged, motivated, and resilient workforce.

High turnover rates are costly for businesses, both in terms of time and money. Coaching can help reduce turnover by increasing employee engagement and job satisfaction. It makes sense, right? When employees feel supported and empowered, they're more likely to stay with your organization and contribute to its success. Coaching can also help reduce stress and overwhelm for employees by providing them with the necessary tools and support they need to do their jobs. As a coaching manager, when you empower employees to take more ownership of their work and development, you'll reduce your own stress levels too, and what manager wouldn't love that? When employees are more autonomous and self-directed, you can focus less on micromanaging and more on other things.

Some businesses hire outside coaches or consultants to improve how their businesses operate and to increase their chances of success. This is good and I've personally experienced benefits from outside coaches, but the one downside is that they can only come around every now and then. It's difficult to access your true potential and that of your people when coaching is only part-time. Think of a professional athlete who spends about 85%-95% of their time working with their coach to prepare for a single event. Once the event has come and gone, they go back to spending the majority of their time preparing for the next event. This method simply will not work in a business where the "event" is taking place every single day. This is why it's so advantageous to have an in-house coach who is present every day, one who is intimately aware of the needs of the business and its people.

Here are a few takeaways:

- ➢ Coaching reduces employee turnover.

- A coaching manager is someone who integrates the principles of coaching, mentoring, and traditional management into their leadership style.

- A coaching manager still provides structure, sets goals, and ensures accountability. However, they do it in a way that empowers employees and encourages them to initiate things independently and own the responsibility.

- They focus on developing their team members' skills, empowering them to take ownership of their work, and supporting their professional growth and development.

- Coaching managers see themselves as facilitators of their team's success, rather than a directive authority figure.

- A coaching manager uses coaching techniques such as active listening, asking powerful questions, and providing constructive feedback to help employees identify their goals, overcome obstacles, and achieve their full potential.

Reminder: there are two primary ways to work with your team:

1. Directive: telling, using your own experience to guide others, mentor, consulting, managing, giving advice.

2. Non-directive: asking questions, active listening, guiding others to find solutions themselves.

Coaching managers blend these two together, hopefully leaning a bit more toward the non-directive approach. Developing a coaching mindset is an ongoing process that requires self-awareness, reflection, and a willingness to learn.

How You Coach Matters

We toss around the word "coaching" frequently these days, but how you define it and the way you actually do it matters. It matters a lot. If you happen to be coaching your people already, do you use any of these methods?

- Threats- i.e. their job, pay, etc.
- Humiliation- calling them out in front of their peers.
- Anger or ridicule.

If you are using any of the above methods, you are not coaching. You are controlling, or are at least attempting to control, your people. This method will never produce a positive, or long-lasting change. You can manage performance to a certain extent, but people need to be coached.

The problem is that a lot of managers, and business owners, only focus on the performance side of the coaching coin. Coaching for performance is important, but the only way lasting change ever takes place is to coach for development. Coaching for performance addresses an individual's skill and technique, while coaching for development addresses the individual.

When you focus only on the performance issue, you are putting all of your attention on the negative results. You can hammer that home till your blue in the face, but it will seldom be effective in bringing about the desired change. This does not mean you ignore poor performance, but rather you seek to correct it by going straight to the source, the individual.

Remember, your personnel roster is filled with actual humans and each one is unique and cannot be reprogrammed like a machine. This is where coaching for development comes into play. Poor performance can almost always be traced to poor habits. If an individual has poor work habits you can teach them new skills, but those skills will not be utilized until their habits have changed.

You will have to tap into the learning style of each person on your team. Developmental coaching focuses on helping a person learn in ways that will keep them growing. It is asking them questions rather than giving them orders and getting them to think instead of giving them step-by-step directions. It is giving them clear goals and holding them accountable for those goals. You want to make them aware of their strengths, and areas in which you can help them grow.

In order to coach someone in a way that will help them grow, you must first develop a relationship built on respect, trust, support, and patience. They must know that you genuinely care about them. If you don't have this kind of relationship with your team, then *that* is your starting point. If you skip this part, or downplay its importance, you will be perceived as fake and insincere.

Here are a few more tips on coaching others:

• Help them become self-aware. Ask open-ended questions that cause them to think about their intentions, performance, and habits. Help them to discover their inconsistencies, instead of pointing them out yourself.

• Encourage them to make progress and recognize their successes.

• Have them set their own goals, and then hold them accountable to their goals.

• Listen to their concerns and allow them to share their feelings.

• Know that change you seek will come, but it won't be overnight.

Remember, both sides of the coin are important. You can coach for performance *and* development at the same time. Do both, and do it consistently, and you will see positive changes that last.

Here are a few more actionable steps for developing the skills and behaviors of a coaching manager:

- Develop Empathy: Be intentional with this and seek to understand the perspectives, motivations, and challenges, of the people on your team.

- Building Trust: Trust is essential for any relationship, and coaching is no different. As a coaching manager, you should work to build trust by being transparent, reliable, and supportive.

- Active Listening: We'll go deeper into this later, but active listening is much more than just. hearing what someone is saying. It involves fully concentrating, understanding what's not being said but implied, and honoring the other person's perspective whether you agree with it or not.

- Asking Questions: Ask open-ended questions that encourage employees to think critically and explore new perspectives. This is about tapping into their innate intelligence and capabilities.

- Provide Constructive Feedback: Give feedback that's specific, timely, and focused on behavior rather than personality. The goal is their growth, not putting the spotlight on errors or mistakes.

If you'll actively work on these things, you're going to grow yourself and your team by leaps and bounds.

Trauma in the Workplace

It's a serious issue and is another important reason why creating a coaching atmosphere within businesses is so vital. I remember reading an article on Forbes that said, "New data suggests that for almost 70% of people, their manager has more impact on their mental health than their therapist or their doctor—and it's equal to the impact of their partner. If you're a leader, you're right to find this data sobering."

Consider this: the average person spends about 90,000 hours at work, and if those hours are a living hell the effect on their mental health can be catastrophic. This is why "business as usual" is no longer going to cut it. We need to radically change how managers manage, and the changes must begin within the ranks of business leaders.

Transitioning managers from an authoritative or traditional approach to a coach-like mindset represents a new, higher standard in leadership and one that benefits both managers and employees. In a coaching atmosphere (aka learning environment) leaders are not just managers but also facilitators of growth and development.

It's great that there are many companies today who do recognize the importance of employee well-being and are taking action. I'm seriously happy about that, but before we upgrade pizza parties and free coffee to yoga mats and complimentary massages, let's address the way employees are treated by leadership

- ✓ Let's upgrade the workplace atmosphere so that innovation and great ideas aren't smothered by the fear of making mistakes and receiving a manager's wrath.

- ✓ Let's recognize the value of people who are consistently high-performers and compensate them accordingly.

- ✓ Rather than only focusing on the objectives of the company, let's tie them to the personal goals of the people doing the work in a spirit of collaboration.

- ✓ Let's access untapped potential by listening to the thoughts and ideas of people working on the frontlines of the business.

While we're on the subject of good mental health, let's not forget about the managers. We can help prevent manager burnout by building actual teams of people that work together towards shared goals, instead of using the term "team" to describe a command-and-control structure where the manger's primary role is to catch the blame for everything that isn't working.

I believe it's possible to create workplaces that are characterized by cooperation, rather than a top-down hierarchy. I've experienced this firsthand. I've witnessed the power of coaching radically change a business (and people's lives) for the better.

Chapter Four

Benefits of a Coaching Style of Leadership

When you're able to connect with your people on a deeper level, actually build a meaningful workplace relationship with them, they're going to do the same with your customers. This is a win/win/win situation. The manager wins. The employees win. And the customers win. And because of that, the business also wins.

As I mentioned in the Introduction, I've personally experienced the transformational power of coaching in my own career when I was co-managing a therapeutic massage studio. As a traditional manager, I often found myself overwhelmed by the demands of managing a team. I was focused on giving direction and solving problems, rather than empowering my team members to find their own solutions. A common misconception is that managers have all the answers, but that simply is not true.

However, after doing a lot of studying and practicing some basic coaching skills, I realized that there was a better way. By adopting a coaching mindset, I was able to shift my focus from telling to asking, from solving to supporting. I learned how to ask powerful questions, listen actively, and provide feedback in a way that inspired growth and development in my team members.

At the time, I didn't even know "coaching managers" was a thing. For me, it was an experiment worth trying because nothing else we tried worked.

Over the next eighteen months we:

- Nearly doubled our number of memberships.

- Transformed the workplace environment to being positive & fun.

- Reduced employee turnover to almost zero.

- Broke all previous sales records.

- Drew attention from corporate and other studios from around the country.

Plus, it actually made my life a lot easier. That's the power of a collaborative atmosphere. As I embraced coaching as part of my role as manager, I found that it wasn't a new skill or tactic, but a new way of being. It requires a certain level of humility. Coaching isn't just a tool to be used in certain situations; it's a mindset that can be applied to all aspects of the job. It's about building trust and rapport with your team members and creating a culture of collaboration and learning. This is an atmosphere that will empower individuals to reach their full potential. A coaching mindset is about creating an environment where individuals can thrive, grow, and succeed.

Adopting a coaching leadership style will have a profound impact on both individuals and organizations. There are many benefits of adopting a coaching style, including increased employee engagement, a more positive workplace atmosphere, improved performance, reduced stress, enhanced communication, development of future leaders, and increased resilience and adaptability.

Let's take a closer look at each of these benefits:

Increased Employee Engagement

When managers take a coaching approach, they empower employees to take ownership of their work and development. This sense of ownership leads to greater engagement, as employees feel more invested in their work and motivated to perform at their best.

A More Positive, Uplifting Workplace Atmosphere

Coaching leaders create a more positive and uplifting workplace atmosphere by focusing on strengths, development, autonomy, and growth. Instead of dwelling on mistakes or shortcomings, coaching leaders celebrate successes and encourage a culture of continuous improvement and learning. This doesn't mean mistakes are ignored or sugar-coated, they're just used as opportunities to learn rather than assigning blame. It's a positive atmosphere that will encourage collaboration, creativity, and innovation, leading to a more vibrant and enjoyable workplace.

Improved Performance

Coaching has been shown to improve performance at both the individual and organizational levels. By asking questions and providing regular feedback, guidance, and support, coaching managers help employees identify areas for improvement and develop strategies to achieve their goals. This focus on development and growth leads to higher performance levels and greater overall success. Not to mention, it leads to increased employee happiness.

Less Stress

Stress is an all-too-common problem in today's workplace, but coaching can help alleviate some of this stress. By providing employees with the tools and support they need to manage their workload, coaching managers help reduce stress and prevent burnout. Bonus: the manager gets this same benefit! This also contributes to a positive and uplifting atmosphere, and who doesn't want more of that?

Improved Communication

Everyone knows that communication is essential for success in any organization, and coaching can help improve communication at all levels. Coaching managers learn to be skilled at active listening, asking powerful questions, and providing constructive feedback, all of which are key components of good communication. By modeling these behaviors, you can help improve communication throughout the entire business.

Develops Future Leaders

Another great thing about a coaching leadership style is that it not only benefits the current workforce but also helps develop future leaders. When your employees are provided with opportunities to grow and develop, you're building a pipeline of talented individuals who will be prepared to take on leadership roles in the future. It's far less expensive to promote employees from within the organization than to hire externally. It saves you from hiring the wrong person, advertising costs, and posting on job boards. Plus, a coaching culture helps attract and retain top talent.

Increased Resilience and Adaptability

Coaching managers help build a culture of resilience and adaptability because employees are encouraged to take risks, try new approaches, and learn from their experiences. They create a safe environment for their people to stretch their abilities and not fear making mistakes.

A coaching approach helps employees feel valued, supported, and motivated, which boosts morale and creates a more uplifting, positive work environment. When employees are engaged and motivated, they're happier and naturally more productive because they're personally invested in their work and strive to reach their goals. Coaching builds loyalty and can reduce turnover. People are far more likely to stay with a company that invests in their growth and development. Wouldn't you?

Some examples of companies who value a coaching culture:

➢ **Google:** Google is known for its coaching culture, where managers are trained to be effective coaches. This approach has helped Google maintain a high level of employee engagement and innovation.

➢ **General Electric:** GE implemented a coaching program for its managers, which resulted in major improvements in employee performance and results for the business.

➢ **IBM:** IBM has a long history of using coaching to develop its leaders. The company attributes much of its success to its coaching culture, which has helped it adapt to changing market conditions and stay competitive.

> **Time etc.** (Leading virtual assistant service in the U.S): This company actually replaced all of their managers with coaches. The result? Employees became 20% more productive and, perhaps more importantly, much happier.

Soft Skills

Multiple books and countless articles have been written about the importance of soft skills in the workplace, and for good reason. Unlike technical skills (aka hard skills) soft skills are what dictate how we work and interact with other people. One could argue that even if an individual possessed an impressive list of technical skills, the odds of them succeeding would be greatly reduced if they didn't also possess empathy, emotional intelligence, kindness, the ability to adapt and effectively communicate.

85% of career success comes from having well-developed soft skills and only 15% from hard skills. That's according to research conducted by Harvard University, the Carnegie Foundation and Stanford Research Center. Granted, that study was published in 1918, but even if the percentages are a little different today, it shows that we've known about the importance of soft skills for well over 100 years.

In 2010, another study by the American Society for Training and Development found that out of the 171.5 billion dollars spent on employee learning and development, only 27.6% went to training on soft skills.

Additionally:

- ➢ A recent report (2023) from Training Magazine found that U.S. companies spent nearly $2 billion on training. I wonder how much of that went to soft skills training.

- ➢ A 2019 LinkedIn report found that 92% of talent professionals said soft skills matter as much, if not more, than hard skills when it comes to hiring. 80% said they're becoming more important to a company's success.

As you can see, most everyone agrees that soft skills (attributes that enable someone to interact harmoniously & effectively with others) are crucial, but can they be taught? I think here is where we can ask a better question:

"Can soft skills be learned?" And the answer is a resounding YES!

But soft skills can't be effectively taught from a book or one-day training courses. They are behavior based so they must be learned in a different way. Of course, an individual must be willing to grow and consciously shape their responses and actions. If this willingness is present, then what that person needs is to work in a coaching environment.

This is why we need Coaching Managers (aka managers who possess and lead with a coaching mindset) who work daily to create a business culture of support and collaboration. It's fairly simple to train people on the technical aspects of their job, but for them to grow and develop strong interpersonal skills, they must work in an atmosphere where such skills are valued and exemplified by their leaders.

We're now in the 21st century, and management styles and techniques of the past are not working, Workplaces today are in crisis. In a 2022 Gallup survey, it was found that employee engagement dropped to a seven-year low. Only a third of workers felt they were engaged at work. Nearly a fifth of workers (18%) stated they were actively disengaged. The measurements for engagement used by

Gallup were made up of several elements, but a few that declined the most were opportunities to learn and grow, clarity of expectations, opportunities to do what they do best, feeling cared about, and connection to the company's purpose.

Feeling trusted, cared about, and supported at work has a significant impact on an employee's level of engagement, their mental health, and their productivity. A coaching manager addresses these concerns head on.

It's worth pointing out that there are some real advantages to creating coaches within the business itself rather than depending solely on outside coaches and consultants. Don't get me wrong, outside coaches and consultants can be extremely valuable and I recommend them highly. As I said in chapter three, I've been coached in this way myself and it was great, but positive changes can happen quicker and be more sustainable when a business has their own in-house coaches on staff. Here are just a few of the advantages of in-house coaches:

- **Cost-Effectiveness:** Training and developing in-house coaches can be more cost-effective in the long run compared to hiring external consultants for coaching services.

- **Internal Understanding**: In-house coaches have a firsthand understanding of the organization's culture, values, and challenges, allowing them to provide more targeted and relevant coaching to employees.

- **Continuous Support:** In-house coaches can provide ongoing support and tailored coaching to employees, which helps build a continuous learning environment within the organization.

- **Builds Internal Capacity:** Developing in-house coaches helps build internal coaching capacity, which makes it possible for the organization to sustain a coaching culture over time. It's kind of like a successful basketball team who has a deep bench of skilled players. If one of the starters has to come out of the game, a skilled sub takes their place, and you don't lose momentum.

- **Tailored Solutions:** In-house coaches can tailor their coaching approach to meet the specific needs and goals of the organization, ensuring a more personalized and effective coaching experience for employees.

- **Increased Engagement:** Employees will be more engaged and responsive to coaching with someone from within the organization, as they may feel more comfortable and connected to the person doing the coaching.

Chapter Five

Common Challenges Transitioning to a Coaching Style

Transitioning to a coaching leadership style can be an exciting journey, but there can be a few challenges too. Let's look at some common challenges that managers may face when transitioning to a coaching leadership style.

Understanding the Benefits

One challenge a manager might face when they're transitioning to a coaching leadership style is not seeing the benefits of coaching. They may not fully grasp how it can improve employee engagement, performance, and overall team interaction. They could also be unsure of how to effectively apply coaching techniques in their day-to-day interactions with their team members.

Rest assured that most everyone feels that way at first. The key is to remain open-minded and start putting into practice what you learn. The quicker you can implement coaching the quicker you'll become comfortable doing it. When you start seeing and experiencing the benefits, you'll be hooked!

Time Constraints

Another common challenge some managers express is time constraints. They may perceive coaching as being time-consuming and could struggle finding the time to engage in coaching conversations amidst their other responsibilities. However, coaching doesn't have to be a lengthy process. Even brief coaching conversations can have a significant impact on an employee's engagement and performance. Be patient with yourself and others. Dedicating just a few minutes a day to coaching conversations will make a huge difference.

Comfort Zone

If you've been a manager for while, you're probably accustomed to a directive or authoritative leadership style. You might feel uncomfortable or uncertain about adopting a more collaborative and empowering coaching approach. These feelings might be more pronounced if you've had some success using traditional leadership styles in the past. This is all normal so don't think you're doing something wrong if you experience these feelings.

We all feel a certain level of discomfort when changing the way we do things. Again, if you can remain open-minded and willing, the feelings will dissipate in time. Especially when you start experiencing positive results.

Resistance to Change

Resistance to change is a common barrier in any organizational transition because humans are just wired that way. We might view change suspiciously, even if there's promise of good things to come. Managers aren't the only ones who might resist change. Employees who have become accustomed to a traditional leadership style may also be skeptical of coaching and could resist the shift to a more collaborative and empowering leadership approach. This is why it's so important for a coaching manager to lead by example and demonstrate the value of coaching through their own actions and behaviors.

One of the biggest challenges you might face when transitioning to a coaching role is letting go of the need to control every aspect of your team's work. Especially if you've been a manager for a long time. It can be difficult to trust that your team will have the skills and knowledge to succeed without your constant oversight.

However, by empowering your team and giving them the freedom to make their own decisions, you will actually create a more resourceful and motivated group of people. Moving to a coaching style of leadership will have certain challenges, but with good support and the right mindset, you can successfully transition and unlock the full potential of your team.

Here are some more tips that will help you:

- Mindset Shift: You could do what I did and take an actual coaching course, or do your own self-study, or attend workshops to help you develop a coaching mindset. There are tons of resources available, and I share a few of them at the end of this book.

- Time Constraints: You can start prioritizing coaching by setting aside dedicated time for coaching sessions and integrating coaching into your daily routine by taking small steps. Be sure to have conversations with your people and let them know what you're doing and why.

- Resistance from Team Members: Address team members' concerns and misconceptions about coaching. Be attentive to their concerns and highlight the benefits they'll receive from coaching.

- Organizational Culture: Advocate for a coaching culture within the organization. This can be a real challenge depending on the mindset of the leaders in the business. Remember, your only job is to educate them on how and why it works, and the benefits they'll enjoy.

- Communicate: Clearly communicate to everyone involved the benefits of coaching and address any concerns or misconceptions they may have.

- Lead by Example: Demonstrate the effectiveness of coaching by embodying coaching principles and incorporating them into your own leadership style. Your behaviors are what reflect this most.

- Involve Team Members: Involve your team members in the coaching process by asking for their input and feedback.

- Seek Support: Seek support from senior management or HR to gain their buy-in and support for creating a coaching culture. Highlight the positive impact coaching can have on employee engagement, performance, and retention.

Don't be discouraged if you run into a few roadblocks, especially in the first stages of the transition. Addressing these challenges and implementing some practical solutions will go a long way toward helping you successfully transition to a coaching style of leadership.

Chapter Six
Everyone Has a Social Style

The most important skill for a leader isn't their ability to manage tasks and projects; it's how well they understand and relate to people. Social Styles, a concept developed by psychologists David Merrill and Roger Reid, offers valuable insights into how individuals communicate and behave in social settings. An understanding of these styles can improve work relationships, collaboration, and team performance. They help you better understand your own social style, how others behave, and most importantly, how to adapt your social style to others so you can work more harmoniously and efficiently.

A keen understanding and practice of the principles of Social Styles is what revolutionized my own approach to management. It was the gateway through which I walked that led me to becoming a coaching manager. I believe it can do the same for you.

What Are Social Styles?

Social Styles are patterns of communication that characterize how individuals interact with others. These styles are based on observable behaviors and can provide valuable insights into how people prefer to communicate, make decisions, and approach tasks. While everyone has a unique blend of styles, most people exhibit one dominant style that influences their behavior in social settings.

The Four Social Styles

Driver Style: needs to control and achieve. Goal oriented. Most comfortable being in charge. Task and tell. All about results and efficiency. Doesn't need all the information to make a decision. Annoyed with delays. Fast-paced and plunges in headfirst.

Expressive Style: likes to be where the action is. Relationship oriented vs task oriented. Wants to be creative and have fun while getting things done. Enthusiastic. Thrives on acknowledgement. Great people skills.

Amiable Style: the most people-oriented of all the styles. Great listeners, great friends, and loyal employees. Team players. Goes along rather than rock the boat. Faced with change, they need time to think it through. Slower making decisions because of their need for security.

Analytical Style: persistent, detail-oriented, high self-expectations, works at slower pace because they want to be accurate and thorough, task-oriented and trends toward perfectionism, good listeners and may ask lots of questions.

Applying Social Styles in Leadership

As a leader, understanding Social Styles can help you tailor your communication and leadership approach to better interact with your team members. Here are some strategies for applying Social Styles in your role as coaching manager:

Adapt Your Style of Communication: Tailor your communication style to match the preferences of your team members. For example, if you are working with an Analytical, provide detailed information and be prepared to answer their questions. If you are working with a Driver, focus on the bottom line and be concise in your communication.

Build Relationships: Recognize the importance of building relationships with your team members. Spend time getting to know them on a personal level and show genuine interest in their well-being. This can help you build trust and rapport, especially with Amiables and Expressives who value interpersonal relationships.

Provide Recognition: Acknowledge and recognize the efforts of your team members, especially Expressives who thrive on acknowledgment. Providing positive feedback and recognition can boost morale and motivation, leading to improved performance.

Facilitate Decision-Making: Understand that different styles may have different approaches to decision-making. For example, Analyticals may prefer a more thorough and data-driven approach, while Drivers may prefer a quicker and more decisive approach. Adapt your decision-making process to accommodate the needs of your team members.

Manage Conflict: Recognize that conflict may arise due to differences in social styles. Be proactive in managing conflict by encouraging open communication and seeking to understand the perspectives of others. Use your knowledge of Social Styles to find common ground and resolve conflicts amicably. Share with your team how you tailor your own communication style when talking to them. Your example will help them learn and use the knowledge of social styles to improve their work relationships.

By identifying the social styles of the people on your team, you can tailor your coaching approach to their style and be more effective. For example, if you're working with a team member who has a dominant social style of communicating, you may need to be more direct and assertive in your coaching approach, while a team member with a more reserved style may require a more supportive and encouraging approach.

Understanding social styles also helps you anticipate potential conflicts or misunderstandings and proactively address them through effective communication and conflict resolution strategies. If you have an opportunity for you and your team to take a personality assessment, such as the DiSC Personality Assessment or the Myers-Briggs Type Indicator, do so. They can be helpful in discovering which social you and your team members lead with in your interactions.

By understanding and leveraging social styles, you will enhance your coaching effectiveness, improve your ability to communicate, and build stronger relationships with their team members. Once you've done this, you will have a foundation upon which you can have coaching conversations with your people.

Remember, coaching is a conversation, or a series of conversations, with another person. And what makes these conversations different is the effect they have on the person being coached.

With that in mind, I want to share a framework that you can use in your coaching conversations. Use this framework as a guide (not strict rules to follow) when discussing something with an employee. It will help keep you in a coaching posture instead of slipping into "fix it" mode.

Coaching Conversation Framework

- Identify the purpose/objective of the conversation.
- Ask questions. Discover their view of the issue.

- Ask what they need from you, or what additional resources they need.

- Reflect back to them what they shared with you. This lets them know you heard and understand their viewpoint.

- Plan for next steps.

Here is an example of the framework in action. It's a conversation between a coaching manager (CM) and an employee named Brittany.

Identify the purpose/objective of the conversation:
CM: Hi Brittany, thank you for meeting with me today. I wanted to discuss the recent project deadline extension. Can you share with me your perspective on what happened and how we can move forward?

Ask questions. Discover their view of the issue:
Brittany: Well, I feel like we were not given enough time to complete the project, considering the additional tasks that were added halfway through. It was pretty stressful trying to meet the original deadline.

CM: I understand. Can you tell me more about the specific challenges you faced during the project?

Brittany: Sure, the additional work required more time and resources than we originally anticipated. This, combined with the tight deadline, made it challenging to deliver quality work.

Ask what they need from you, or what additional resources they need:
CM: Thank you for sharing that. What support or resources do you think you needed to help you meet the original deadline?

Brittany: I think having more clarity on priorities and additional team members to share the workload would have been helpful.

Reflect back to them what they shared with you:
CM: So, it sounds like you feel that the project deadline was challenging due to the unexpected extra work and the need for more people and resources. Is that correct?

Brittany: Yes, that's right. I believe with more time and support we could have delivered a better outcome.

Plan for next steps:

CM: Moving forward, let's work together to ensure clearer communication on project priorities and timelines. I'll also look into allocating any additional resources needed to support the team. How does that sound to you?

Brittany: That sounds great. I appreciate your support and understanding.

CM: Of course, I'm here to support you. Let's schedule a follow-up meeting next week to check on the progress. Does that work for you?

Brittany: Yes, that works for me. Thank you.

CM: Thank you, Brittany. I appreciate your openness and willingness to help us all improve. Let's continue working together to ensure the success of this project.

Notice how the two worked together to arrive at the answers they needed, and what their next steps would be. Also notice how the manager didn't slip into "fix it" mode or try to find someone to blame.

Chapter Seven

Active Listening and Why It's a Crucial Skill

You may be a good listener, but **active listening** is a whole other level. I first studied this in a meaningful way when taking a coaching certification course. I have always thought of myself as a good listener, but in truth I had only scratched the surface when it comes to truly listening to another person. It was during that coaching course where I first learned about the work of Nancy Kline, who pioneered the development of *The Thinking Environment* and is the founder of Time to Think. I encourage you to check out her work to learn how powerful the art of active listening can be.

Active listening is when you not only hear what someone is saying, but also tune in to their thoughts and feelings. It's being able to "read between the lines" and hear what they're trying to convey, even if their words are expressing something else. It turns a one-way conversation into a two-way, deeply meaningful interaction.

Active listening is a transformational experience, and to paraphrase Ms. Kline, "The best plan emerges from the client's best thinking, from their stories, and from the quality of their relationship with you. Transformative listening is a central part of this success." In this case, the "client" would whichever person on your team that you're having a conversation with. In other words, your people will do their best thinking when you create a "thinking environment" through deep listening.

Active Listening Dos & Don'ts

DO:

- Listen for ideas and emotions, not just words.
- Limit your own talking.
- Be more interested in what they're thinking than sharing what you're thinking.
- Consider it a success when they come up with better ideas than yours.
- Understand that pre-conceived assumptions will block communication.
- Ask what else they're thinking and feeling. And ask again, and then again.

- Let them know you want to hear them and will not interrupt.

DON'T:
- Interrupt them while they're sharing what they're thinking and feeling.
- Assume you know more, or that you can think for them.
- Simply wait your turn to speak, rather than truly wanting to know what they think.
- Tell them what they're thinking and feeling.
- Try to "fix" them, or assume they need fixing in the first place.
- Think their perception is wrong. Accurate or not, it's their perception in the moment.
- Immediately speak when they become silent. They could still be trying to put what they feel into words. Give them the gift of space.

Have you ever had a conversation when you wondered if the other person was listening to what you were saying? You probably wondered if your message was getting through, or if you should just stop talking. It can feel like you're talking to a brick wall. Now, imagine that at some point in the past there may have been a time when someone talking to you felt the same way. Yikes! You can see how this could lead to some problems, especially if you're in a position of leadership.

By becoming a better listener, you'll improve your ability to positively influence others and even avoid potential conflicts and misunderstandings. Plus, active listening builds trust and stronger relationships. It's okay if it doesn't feel natural at first, it's a skill that can be practiced and improved over time.

Chapter Eight

Why Caring Leadership Matters

Some of the best leaders I've met were people who never sought out leadership roles in the first place. What was it about these individuals that led them to eventually be regarded as exceptional leaders?

They cared.

It was their innate qualities, such as integrity, empathy, and a genuine concern for others' well-being, that naturally drew people to them. They're people who lead by example, inspiring those around them to work toward common goals and strive for excellence. Even though they didn't actively seek leadership positions, their ability to connect with others and their strong sense of purpose propelled them to become respected and influential leaders.

If you've been in the workforce for some time, chances are you've worked for a narcissistic leader at some point. They're easy to spot due to their self-centered behavior, constant need for admiration, arrogance, and tendency to take all the credit for themselves while giving all of the blame to others. In cases like this, it doesn't matter how many hard skills one has because a toxic work environment created by a narcissistic leader will undermine employee productivity and morale, making it a challenge (at best) to succeed regardless of how talented the rest of the team may be. Some are quieter about it than others, but the negative effects of these types of leaders are the same.

Teddy Roosevelt once said,

> *"Nobody cares how much you know until they know how much you care."*

Nowhere is that more applicable than the workplace. And again, if you've been working for a long time, I bet you've had for a leader for whom you would move mountains if they asked. I'd also bet that you had no question whether or not that leader cared about you, supported you, and had your back in a crisis.

Caring will always precede connection and caring behaviors are fundamental to establishing meaningful workplace relationships. Few things things—if any— matter more because without good connections, the culture of the workplace unravels. A narcissistic leader creates a culture where actions are driven by fear or obligation, whereas a caring leader creates a culture where actions are fueled by people's genuine desire to succeed.

I share these things because the only way a manager, supervisor, or business owner can embody a coaching mindset and create a coaching atmosphere in their business is if they truly care for other people. You see, coaching isn't a slick business tactic, shortcut, or hack that can be deployed for immediate results; it's a process of transformation that requires genuine care, dedication, and a commitment to long-term growth and development. You can't "fake it till you make it" when it comes to a caring, coaching mindset.

The truth is leadership is much more than a position of authority; it's a profound act of service. Leaders dedicate themselves to the growth, development, and well-being of those they lead. They prioritize the needs of their team, and do their best to guide them toward success, not just in the eyes of the business, but also by supporting their personal and professional goals.

This commitment to service requires empathy, humility, and a genuine desire to make a positive impact.

Caring leaders understand that their role is not about personal gain or recognition; it's about selflessly serving others and creating a culture of support, growth, and excellence. In essence, leadership is an endeavor that demands a deep sense of responsibility and a genuine care for the people you lead.

What characteristics must one possess in order to positively influence, inspire, and guide others? Here are a few qualities that stand out to me from my own experience.

Humility

A leader with humility creates an environment where others feel safe and can contribute their ideas without fear of ridicule. They know the key is to be a problem-solver and willing to work with others to create solutions. A genuine leader will then share the credit with everyone involved. They prioritize the needs of the team over their own personal goals and ego. Humble leaders are open to feedback and seek out ways to improve themselves and their organization.

Empathy

The best leaders work to understand and relate to the

emotions and experiences of their team members. They know that the decisions they make have an impact on others. They work toward creating a supportive and inclusive work environment where everyone feels valued and heard. They invest time in getting to know the individuals on their team so they can better communicate with them and build stronger relationships.

Self-awareness

A caring leader is aware of both their strengths and their weaknesses. They're confident in their skills but are willing to acknowledge areas where they need growth. This quality is crucial for the leader who must hire a team to help them accomplish a specific goal. By having clarity about their own skills and traits, they have more clarity on what to look for when hiring new people. Self-aware leaders are better equipped to make decisions that align with their values and vision.

Visionary

A leader with vision is clear on the direction they're going and knows what they want to accomplish. They have a clear and inspiring vision for the future and are able to communicate that vision to their team. They tend to be passionate and relentless in the pursuit of their goal, yet understand they need help from others. Visionary leaders are able to motivate and inspire others to work towards a common goal. They also have a strong sense of purpose and are able to create a sense of meaning and fulfillment for their team.

Decisive

An effective leader has a clear understanding of their priorities and is able to act quickly when necessary. Decisive leaders gather information and weigh the pros and cons of different options before choosing a course of action. They understand that decisions made without hesitation, and made at the right time, are necessary in order to accomplish things. Additionally, a wise leader will be open to the counsel of others. They'll still be the one making the decision, but after having acquired as much information and perspective as possible.

Optimistic

The most influential leaders are a consistent source of positive energy. They exude hope and confidence about the future and do so openly and often. They communicate well with others, and don't allow negativity to gain a foothold. Optimistic leaders have a positive attitude and are able to maintain a sense of hope and resilience even in difficult times. They're able to inspire their team and create a sense of optimism and possibility in the face of challenges. Optimistic leaders are solution oriented, and work to turn setbacks into opportunities.

This isn't an exhaustive list and there are many traits that make up a truly great leader. However, the qualities listed here are a solid foundation on which leaders can build so they can lead themselves, and others, to greatness.

Perhaps the most important thing to remember is that leaders are human beings too. They have all the same feelings and emotions as everyone else and they can't be expected to operate as a machine.

If you're in a position of leadership, I encourage you to be kind to yourself. Strive for excellence and deeper levels of self-awareness, but please don't put yourself under a microscope and expect perfection 24/7. You're going to make mistakes. Own them and move on. You're not going to exhibit the above qualities to the same degree every day. The important things are consistency and transparency.

When the people you lead see you owning mistakes, not hiding behind a fabricated image or ego, they will empathize with you. They'll learn that mistakes aren't the end of the world when they see you bounce back with a solution. When they observe your optimism in the midst of challenges, they'll learn that tough times are temporary. Your position isn't about authority as much as it's about example. This is genuine leadership and will inspire your team more than you might imagine.

A Paradox?

It's important to address a common misconception that has caused innumerable problems in thousands of businesses around the world, which is: great employees don't always make great managers. I'd even go so far as to say that they're seldom great at management—at least not at first.

This is something I learned the hard way after years of working in various businesses. While I could recount numerous horror stories from my personal experiences involving once stellar employees who became bad managers, the story that should be shared is my own. Yes,

I was one of those high-performing employees who was asked to be a manager. In fact, that happened on more than one occasion and in different businesses in which I worked. Of course, I made all the same mistakes most new managers make:

- I tried being everyone's best friend.

- I assumed everyone would automatically care as much as I did.

- I believed if I understood what needed to be done, everyone else did too.

- I tried cheerleading the team to success.

- I attempted the carrot and stick approach, aka reward and punishment.

- I tried ruling with an iron fist.

- I believed not pleasing everyone all of the time meant I was failing.

You get the idea. As you might have guessed, nothing on the above list worked. I understand the assumption that exceptional employees will naturally evolve into outstanding managers, but it's a flawed belief. Even as an employee, I believed that since I was very successful as an employee, I would naturally be a great manager. I was wrong. High-performing individuals do contribute significantly to the success of a team, but the transition from being an excellent employee to being an excellent manager doesn't happen automatically or by chance, it must be an intentional process that's embraced equally by both employer and employee.

Different Skill Sets

In hindsight, it's easy for me to see why being a high-performing employee doesn't translate into a high-performing manager. The skills that make an employee excel at their job are likely much different than the core skills needed by an effective manager. A star employee might possess exceptional problem-solving skills (as it relates to their role), attention to detail, and technical abilities, but a manager requires a broader set of qualities. Communication, active listening, leadership, conflict resolution, and strategic thinking are crucial when guiding a group of individuals to work as a team.

Interpersonal Skills

Another common pitfall for an employee transitioning to management is a lack of interpersonal skills, and the way in which they relate to others in the workplace. Excelling in a role often focused on individual achievements may not equip someone with the ability to understand and motivate a team with diverse thoughts and viewpoints. The transition to managing people requires a mindset shift from self-reliance to understanding and leveraging the strengths of other people in ways that will lead to collaboration and quickly resolved conflicts.

Delegation and Adapting to Change

When you have an employee who is used to handling their own tasks with great skill and dedication, they might struggle with delegating work to others—or even worse, they might become a micromanager because they're used to doing everything themselves. Managers must learn to delegate tasks based on team members' strengths and then trust them to deliver positive results.

When changes occur, expected or not, a manager must quickly adapt themselves and then lead their team through periods of uncertainty, while also making decisions that will affect their entire team. That could be a challenge for someone who is accustomed to a more predictable work routine.

Good News!

The good news is great employees can become great managers. To illustrate that point, I'd like to share a story with you. I began this article by telling you about the many mistakes I made during my first ventures into the world of management, but thankfully my story didn't end there. I was fortunate to eventually work for an employer who understood that even though I was rocking it as an employee, I'd need some help to become a great manager. They hired a business coach whose specialty was preparing individuals for management. I worked with that coach for more than two years, and like a sponge, I absorbed everything I learned.

The business was a thriving therapeutic massage studio, and my job as manager was to hire and train front desk staff. I was also tasked with growing the membership, which had been stagnant for more than two years. With coaching, I grew by leaps and bounds, and I wanted to build a team that loved working together, made more money for themselves, and looked forward to going to work. It took a little over a year to work out the kinks and implement changes, but we grew that membership so much and so fast that the owner began thinking they'd have to expand in order to accommodate all the new clients. Owners of other franchises from across the country (USA) began calling us to ask the "secret" of our success.

I had finally learned what it meant to be a great manager, but I don't deserve the credit for our record-breaking success, my team did that. My role in it was to be more coach than manager, allow my team to use their strengths, trust them to deliver results, and get out of their way. Maybe that's the most important lesson of all: A great manager helps others grow and flourish.

If you're an employer who's thinking of moving one of your high-performing employees into a management position, do it! The character traits that helped them become a star in your organization can also help them become an amazing manager. The key is not abandoning them during the transition and assuming they know how to transfer their drive and dedication to a managerial role.

I also recommend finding a great coach who can help guide them into a different mindset. Give them room to grow and make mistakes, and then watch them soar.

5 Hot Tips for Developing a Coaching Mindset

1. Be Transparent

Trust is built on honest and open communication. Let your team know you intend to become more coach-like. Shifting from a direct management style to a coaching style might freak them out. Especially if they're used to you being the source of all answers and decisions.

2. More Asking, Less Telling

Change your communication style. Instead of supplying all the answers, ask questions like, "How do you think this should be handled?" or "Is there another way we could approach this situation?" This encourages your team to think for themselves, look for solutions, and take ownership.

3. More Listening, Less Talking

Active listening: it's a conscious effort to actually hear what the other person is saying and understand their perspective without judgement or harsh criticism. This helps them feel safe coming to you with their thoughts and ideas.

4. Create a Safe & Positive Environment

As mentioned above, this starts with really listening. Allow open communication and give them room to learn and make mistakes. People who fear making mistakes at work will never grow beyond their present state. Celebrate wins, coach through the losses.

5. Recognize Individual Strengths

A coaching manager recognizes that each person has their unique skills, abilities, and expertise. Assign tasks that align with those strengths. This will fuel their confidence and development as well as overall team success.

Coaching Questions Examples

Good coaching questions will help you learn more about your team members, understand their perspectives, and help them flourish. Below are sixteen examples of the kind of questions you could use.

Remember: Use the ***COACHING CONVERSATION FRAMEWORK**

- What might have brought you to that decision?
- What options do you have?
- Are there other opportunities here you'd like to pursue?
- What might be the results of those options?
- Are you able to use your strengths in your role?
- How can we better utilize your strengths?
- What work goals do you want to achieve?
- What would you like to see happen with (current project or activity)?
- How do you think this should be done?

- What's the actual problem you're trying to solve?
- What is something you would like to change?
- What do you need from me?
- How else can we get this done?
- What other resources do you need?
- How can I support you?
- What matters most to you at work?

*Coaching Conversation Framework

1. Identify the purpose/objective of the conversation.
2. Ask questions. Discover their view of the issue.
3. Ask what they need from you, or what additional resources they need.
4. Reflect back to them what they shared with you. This lets them know you hear and understand their viewpoint.
5. Plan for next steps.

Assessing Your Coaching Mindset

Instructions:

For each statement, indicate whether it applies to you (Yes/No).

- ➤ Do you actively demonstrate tasks or assignments to your team members when appropriate? Yes/No

- ➤ Do you prioritize listening to your employees' perspectives before suggesting solutions or courses of action? Yes/No

- ➤ Do you wait to hire the right person for an open position rather than hiring just anyone? Yes/No

- ➤ When performance does not meet expectations, do you clarify expectations and enforce consequences of nonperformance? Yes/No

> Are you consistent in recognizing good work and providing specific feedback on why their performance was good? Yes/No

> Do you actively welcome ideas and suggestions from members of your team? Yes/No

> Do you work with staff to build a development plan, seeking their recommendations and coaching as needed? Yes/No

> Do your staff meetings occur on a scheduled calendar and follow a standardized agenda organized around department and organizational goals? Yes/No

> Do you regularly check in with your employees, noting what's working well and documenting areas needing attention for follow-up? Yes/No

> Do you use a defined process for cascading communication from the organization or within your department to all team members? Yes/No

- When asking employees to change behaviors, do you explain how this makes a difference for the team, organizational goals, and direction? Yes/No

- Do your staff feel that you role-model the standards of behavior that you expect of them? Yes/No

- Are you comfortable with periods of silence during conversations with your team members? Yes/No

- Do you regularly provide feedback to your team members on their performance and behavior, highlighting both strengths and areas for improvement? Yes/No

- Do you involve your team members in problem-solving and decision-making processes, allowing them to contribute their ideas and perspectives? Yes/No

➢ Do you encourage a culture of continuous learning and development within your team, supporting employees in acquiring new skills and knowledge? Yes/No

➢ Do you actively seek and consider feedback from your team members on your own leadership style and areas for improvement? Yes/No

➢ Do you prioritize building strong, trusting relationships with your team members, recognizing the importance of rapport in effective leadership? Yes/No

➢ Do you provide opportunities for your team members to take on new challenges and responsibilities, fostering their growth and development? Yes/No

➢ Do you demonstrate empathy and understanding towards your team members, recognizing, and acknowledging their individual needs and circumstances? Yes/No

➤ Do you communicate openly and transparently with your team members, sharing information about organizational goals, challenges, and changes? Yes/No

➤ Do you actively listen to your team members, seeking to understand their perspectives and concerns before offering solutions or guidance? Yes/No

➤ Do you promote a positive and inclusive work environment, valuing diversity and creating opportunities for all team members to contribute and succeed? Yes/No

➤ Do you hold yourself accountable for your actions and decisions, setting a positive example for your team members to follow? Yes/No

➤ Do you encourage creativity and innovation within your team, supporting new ideas and approaches to problem-solving? Yes/No

➢ Do you recognize and celebrate the achievements and successes of your team members, showing appreciation for their hard work and dedication? Yes/No

➢ Do you prioritize the well-being and work-life balance of your team members, recognizing the importance of their health and happiness? Yes/No

Interpretation:

- Count the number of "Yes" responses.
- The more "Yes" responses, the more aligned your mindset is with coaching principles.

If you answered "yes" 20 or more times: Congratulations! You have merged the traits of manager and coach into one powerful role. You actively coach employees towards higher performance and hold them (and yourself) accountable. Employees understand how their performance makes a difference and aligns to the overall business performance. Continue to lead by example and create opportunities for others to grow and develop!

If you answered "yes" 15 - 19 times: Your role of "Coaching Manager" is emerging. Continue to focus on clear communication, active listening, and clear expectations. Be as transparent as possible with your team and acknowledge their contributions.

14 or fewer times: Your role of "Coaching Manager" is underway, but maybe not well defined quite yet. Take initiative by stepping up your communication with your team. Remember, coaching is a series of conversations with other people. Good rapport, respect, and trust are built on great communication. You're on your way so keep going!

You Make a Bigger Difference Than You Think

Can changing the workplace change the world? I believe it can. It may not solve every problem, but it will spark positive changes in many ways.

- ➢ The Great Resignation

- ➢ Labor shortages in healthcare, manufacturing, hospitality, skilled trades, and many more.

- ➢ Hundreds (if not thousands) of social media sites dedicated to people who hate their jobs.

There are reasons for all of these things, and it isn't because younger generations are lazy or simply do not want to work. The issues affect all generations currently in the workforce. Not to mention that there's a worldwide mental health crisis and the world seems to have gone crazy all around us. Everyone feels this, is affected by it, and they're going to work burdened with it. We can't expect people to come to work and check their feelings at the door. More and more people are suffering and burning out, and while we may not be able to address all their needs in the workplace, we can at least not add to their suffering. Work life and home life don't exist independently of one another. It's all life, and we can do our part to ensure that the cultures of our businesses are uplifting and encouraging, as they develop and support those who spend a large part of their lives there.

Think about this: the average person spends 90,000 hours of their life at work. Who wants to spend those hours in a cutthroat environment where they're undervalued and unappreciated with little chance of advancing their own goals?

Old paradigms are finally dying. Command-and-control environments and the reward/punishment model where you're often told, "You're lucky to have a job" simply isn't going to work anymore—and it never should have in the first place.

The great news: This is being recognized. There are people like you who are actively working to create a new kind of workplace environment where collaboration, kindness, empathy, employee development, increased employee engagement—and even happiness—are top priorities. A happy employee is a person who is more fulfilled and enjoys their work. They'll go home to their families in a better state of mind. They'll show up in the world differently.

Recommended Reading

The Coaching Manual
by Julie Starr

The Coaches' Handbook
by Jonathan Passmore

Becoming a Coach: The Essential ICF Guide
by Jonathan Passmore & Tracy Sinclair

Coaching for Performance: The Principles and Practice of Coaching and Leadership
by Sir John Whitmore

Co-Active Coaching: New Skills for Coaching People Toward Success in Work and Life
by Laura Whitworth, Karen Kimsey-House, Henry Kimsey-House, and Phillip Sandahl

Keith has spent more than thirty years on the frontlines of multiple businesses, serving in both employee and management positions. His philosophies have been featured on The Dr. Julie Show, All Things Connected, on Empower Radio as well as Internet TV show, Mental Shift with Michelle Mras.

He's a Certified Integrative Coach, and the author of six books, including Your Time Is Now, a book about personal transformation and reaching one's maximum potential. He currently travels the United States as a nomad, coaching and mentoring others in their quest to reach their full potential and accomplish transformative goals. Check out his website at StraightUpLiving.com.

www.ingramcontent.com/pod-product-compliance
Lightning Source LLC
Chambersburg PA
CBHW050327230526
45471CB00005B/2389